How LinkedIn Solved My Mid-Life Crisis
and
How It Can Grow Your Business

How LinkedIn Solved My Mid-Life Crisis
and
How It Can Grow Your Business

written by

Tony K Silver

Edited by: AnnMarie Wyncoll

Begin-A-Book (www.beginabook.com)

Contents

Contents

Acknowledgements

There are many people without whom this book would not be possible and a few I'd like to specifically thank -

Mark Perl - LinkedIn Expert
Warren Cass - Entrepreneur
David Hyner - Mentor, Mastermind Coach and all round top guy!

Stephanie Silver - Wife and Lead Support
Buster - Four Legged Friend and Daily Companion

Your support, contributions and general good advice have helped me not only produce this book, but to be who I am and where I am today.

And to my readers, past, present and future...thank you.

Tony K Silver

INTRODUCTION AND MY STORY

y midlife crisis came about at the age of forty-eight. I was in a job I joyed, I had financial security. Life for me and my family was good.

hen, one day, the first of several curveballs (for which I was woefully unprepared) me hurtling my way. Balls that would hit me square in the face. Balls I uld subsequently learn to duck and eventually balls I would expertly catch.

ere is my story.

1at day started out like any other day, battling the traffic as I drove to ork in West London. There was nothing out of the ordinary, nothing to ert me to what was about to happen, when I arrived at the office early. As Senior Account Director, I had the flexibility to work the hours I needed which suited me perfectly. Though the job was target based I was doing :ll, and in that period was on course to invoice triple my target which uated to a substantial seven figure sum. It was the best job I'd ever had.

ound mid-morning I received an 'all-staff' email, requesting that we be on e shop floor at 11am - there was to be an announcement from the Managing irector. Speculation was rife and our worst fears were realised when it s announced that following due process, redundancies would be made. To y it put everyone on edge for the next few days was an understatement. rentually, those at risk were informed. I was not on the list. This time.

1ree months later another 'all staff' email arrived and now I wasn't so :ky. I was on the list. After going through the 'due process' I was informed at I hadn't survived.

:an still remember that moment as if it was yesterday - indeed I have a r in my eye as I write this. I recall phoning my wife to let her know and tening helplessly as she broke down. It was one of the worst experiences my life.

ter that meeting, driving back to my family, I went through a series of 1otions: anger, blame, frustration, sadness, fear, and trepidation.

Trepidation of what was to come, and of seeing my wife. I didn't know ho
I would deal with what I knew would be an emotionally charged meeting

Arriving home, I tried to be resolute, but it was useless. Tears flowed free
as I hugged my sobbing wife and recognised this as an all-time low point
was utterly destroyed.

The conversation with my wife was a series of challenging emotions bu
in a strange way, I also understood the Managing Director's decision. I h
been a director of another business for the previous ten years and knew th
change had to happen for businesses to survive.

It didn't stop me from having a pity party first though.

My advice, looking back, is to get those emotions out, have the pity par
blame anyone and everyone, but then realise the only person who has a
real bearing on this situation is you. You need to own the situation and
do that you have to get the negativity out of your system. Only then can y
start planning how you're going to turn things around.

My main concern was financial. I was the primary earner and though
been a junior partner (25% owner) in another company for ten years, th
had also ended - and not well. I'd invested financially in the business but w
given an unfair ultimatum which left me with no other option than to qu
I forfeited a large sum of money and lost my initial investment. Sudder
there were no savings, no income, and no job but we still had outgoings
realised we needed help and fast.

Fortunately, I'd had the foresight to arrange mortgage insurance whi
meant six months' payments were partially covered - but that was it. M
wife's salary was not going to support us…there was no choice. I had to si
on.

The money you get on the dole is minimal and I felt desperate and in fa
useless at this point. I was given some great advice though; that I should
be ashamed of my situation - I should be honest and own it.

With this in mind I told my creditors of the situation and mostly they we
understanding. Various payment holidays were agreed, and I felt my stre
reduce.

One vital fact I have omitted thus far is the year. Why? Because it was 2008. The year of the recession. I knew that finding a new job during this time would be incredibly challenging, not least because I was also forty-eight years old. Allegedly, ageism doesn't exist, but I can tell you it did and still does; something that makes me incredibly angry.

So here I was, potentially too old to find a job in a recession where jobs were sparse. Further, salaries seemed to have dropped whilst unscrupulous companies took advantage of the situation. Looking at our budget showed a dark picture indeed - even with the measures I had put in place. Anxiety set in.

I recognised I needed a plan. After a month of frustration, I finally came across a local executive job club. A charity run by volunteers with the aim of helping executives – like me – to find work. How? By offering re-training. This was a turning point.

The first two weeks I was advised to continue what I had been doing up until now and report back. I'm proud to say I was praised both weeks on my effort. I was putting in a full working week looking for a job and this in itself had become a job.

Then in week three the bombshells fell. I learnt that 70% of the positions I was looking at didn't even exist, so the normal routes to the job market were of little use. Joining all those recruitment boards, sending off my CV and touring the many business estates in the area had been virtually pointless.

There were some positives though, two in fact:

> We needed to use LinkedIn; and
> We needed to go networking

Having been on LinkedIn since 2006 I understood the concept of using this, but networking? I didn't even know what that was.

I soon learned that networking involved meeting other businesspeople at various times of the day (but mainly early breakfast) with a view to building relationships and helping each other with your individual goals.

I needed to know more, like where were these meetings, how often and what was the format? At the same time, I had begun to realise that simply being 'on' LinkedIn wasn't enough. I actually had to use it.

The job club had charity status at the Thames Valley Chamber of Commerce which meant there were free networking places up for grabs. 'Free' worked for my budget so I took up the offer and a few days later arrived at a local hotel to meet more than sixty suited businesspeople. To say it was terrifying is an understatement. When I got home, I was anxious and depressed. If this was one of the ways to market myself then I was going to struggle. I was scared, I felt like crying, but I knew that would serve no purpose.

I returned to the networking meeting the following month but with one subtle change. After my first experience I'd had a chat with some of the guys who ran the job club and asked if I could have some business cards that I could add my name to. I planned to hand these out at the next event therefore representing the job club as well as myself. They were more than happy to oblige, and I soon had a small supply.

The outcome was incredible. People were interested in the job club concept, some even eager to help and I was able to inform them I was one of those looking for work with the support of the club. I began to be invited to many other networking groups as a guest. I could hardly believe the change in fortune.

As time went on, I discovered that the Thames Valley networking scene was vibrant but often, there was an investment required. Some of the groups had a membership fee and most had an attendance cost. I needed to find a strategy which minimalised my outlay, so I used free passes as often as I could. Some groups were generous enough to waive the membership fee and occasionally other great networkers paid for me to go, but this could not continue indefinitely. I needed another plan.

In a moment of blinding clarity, I realised I could leverage bartering trading in its oldest form – and it worked.

Having run my own company, I realised I had knowledge I could swap and people I could refer my fellow networkers to – and vice versa. Before long I had collected a good network and become a key referrer.

other tactic I discovered was to offer to help run a networking group ch automatically gave me free access. This became a great way of growing connections.

ney, it transpires, is not the only currency. You just need to be inventive.

working became a big part of my activity (and remains so to this day) what about LinkedIn? Which is, after all, the point of this book.

a Chamber of Commerce event, I was fortunate to meet a LinkedIn ner who delivered a brilliant session on how to use the platform. I stayed ind, got chatting and as a result he took me under his wing. With his lance I learned how to set up my profile, how to engage with others and to use all the various functions. He was also kind enough to connect me ome great people and continued to provide help and support.

more time I spent on LinkedIn, the more I realised how powerful a ing tool it was and that most users were unaware of how to maximise its efits. I had a feeling LinkedIn was about to become a big part of my life, st didn't quite know how big.

months passed and funds became tight. All financial coverage on the tgage had expired and I owed money. I was very open and honest with se to whom I was in debt and as a result the majority were fair to me eturn. My only revenue stream at that time was job seekers allowance ch was not enough. The pressure grew.

coming months were hard, but I chose to remain optimistic and even iplined when it came to networking and job hunting. I always had a plan a to do list – even down to what I would wear (shirt and tie) if I secured nterview.

ntually my persistence paid off and I was given an interview at the mber of Commerce – the one that had played a role in my earlier journey.

tended, determined to make a good impression, and left forty-five utes later with a job offer and a start date of the following Monday.

relief was immense.

The job I had secured was a sales role with commission, but I soon learn that it was a flawed commission system and rarely achievable. Though I w top salesperson regularly, the commission did not reflect this and person turnover in the whole department was very poor. My money worries w far from over.

Spotting an opportunity, I began to barter again, in the way I had w networking, but this time it was for roles within the Chamber. I managed obtain a new job in the Events Team which eased things a little financia and any income (such as travel expenses) that I didn't use, I put away i savings. Slowly I began to feel more financially secure. I continued to k my creditors up to date and again was able to negotiate some leeway. Be upfront, I found, meant there was always a way.

The role in the events team gave me the opportunity to network more a bonus, I was paid to do so. In the end I stayed in that job for three and I years which was enjoyable - for the most part.

An unexpected benefit to this new way of life was an improvement my work/life balance. A lot of the networking and events took place o breakfast so I would often be finished by 2.00pm. This gave me time myself and to my family – a luxury that had been scarce before.

By the time I left the events department I had worked on over four hund projects. I had networked throughout the Thames Valley and attended so elite corporate functions. I had met with top directors and often been sea next to them as we enjoyed lively conversation around football, child pets, and LinkedIn. I am fortunate to still call some of these directors friends.

Sadly, when the CEO of the Chamber passed away, I was informed my role was no longer required. An alternative was offered but it took so negotiation (again) before I was eventually interviewed for a job wh matched my skills and maintained a similar level of financial security. job was in the Export department.

At first, I was excited. I needed to learn new skills and pass exams which something I embraced and relished. The reality was, however, tedious, I found myself in a downward spiral. Occupational Health stepped in doctors prescribed anti-depressants.

The beginning of the end came during a meeting with a chap I had known a few years who basically told me I had to get out, but that I needed a plan. He would help me, he said.

The plan involved finding a niche, getting some money behind me to cover that first year and to get good people who I could buy services from. That way I could network and offer support and expertise in several fields, not just my own. After almost 8 months I had secured enough income to be able to leave my job at the Chamber. Handing in my notice gave me a huge sense of release.

I look back on this period of my life and realise it taught me a lot, not least that I could leave the corporate world and branch out on my own. I am now very happy doing something I really enjoy with the knowledge that I am financially secure for years to come.

It might feel as if you are stepping outside your comfort zone, but if you are able to take a leap of faith, sometimes it can really pay off.

LINKEDIN - WHAT'S IT ALL ABOUT?

inkedIn is the platform used by most business to business (B2B) companies
well as some that are business to consumer (B2C). It's also a personal
atform that was devised by the human resources (HR) industry, and for
any years was just an online curriculum vitae (CV). That was back in 2004
d it remained unchanged for the next 7 years.

round 2011, sizeable companies began to explore LinkedIn and found
at as a large and rapidly growing database, it had a lot of useful features.
ements that could assist in areas such as marketing, for example. It wasn't
ng before the smaller companies caught on and the platform became more
idely used. The 'groups' feature in particular, became very powerful.

2016 there were huge changes. Microsoft acquired LinkedIn and updated
e platform – some of which was not, in my opinion, for the better. Super
ers like me found sections we had utilised a lot, removed or edited though
me of those (such as groups) are starting to make a comeback.

18 saw another major change although this was not by LinkedIn itself, but
its users. There was a significant shift in how the platform was perceived,
d once again it became a serious business tool, not just another social
edia platform.

day, this remains the case although there are some elements of 'social
edia' creeping back in which is not necessarily a bad thing. It is still
imarily a business platform though, which means your LinkedIn profile is
extremely important part of your presence. Here you can tell the world
hat is important to you and what you want them to know, so we will now
ver how to set up your profile for best results.

he first thing you need to understand is that your profile has to be engaging
r the viewer which means it must be about them.

onfused?

u might wonder why when it's your profile. Let me explain:

Your LinkedIn profile is split into two parts, **(A)** and **(B)**. These two parts are then divided into sections, **four** of which will be visible to anyone who views your profile or searches for you.

These four sections are found in part (A) of your profile (above the fold in old parlance) and comprise:

- The Banner
- Your Headshot
- Your Headline
- The first 3 lines of your '**About**' section

It is therefore key to optimise these sections, not only for maximum visibility to other users, but also to ensure the LinkedIn algorithm knows how best to promote you.

We will look at each of these four sections in more detail but first, a quick note about **Keywords** and **Connections** which, for me, are the cornerstone of the platform.

KEYWORDS
Defining Your Keywords

s is a vital task and one I always ask my clients to undertake. The words you choose to add to your profile, will directly affect results in ns of your overall visibility to other platform users. Applied correctly, words will also distinguish you from other professionals in your field.

ou have a generic keyword (e.g., coach), for example, your profile will ure alongside many other users. This means you will be competing for ntion in too large a pond.

lly, the keywords you use should filter you into a pool of 10,000 maximum the UK), so you need two or three words that will achieve this.

How to find your keywords

research your keywords:

Type a suitable keyword into the search box at the top of LinkedIn and press enter. My keyword, for example, is '**LinkedIn Profiler**'.

On the next page click on '**People**'. This will list all the LinkedIn users who have that keyword in their profile. At the time of writing (July 2021), this generated 3,700 results for those with '**LinkedIn Profiler**' on their page.

Next, narrow down your search by location. Click on the '**Location**' icon at the top and choose from the drop-down menu. Selecting '**United Kingdom**' has reduced the number in my search for '**LinkedIn Profiler**' to **173**. As this is a low number, I know that using the '**LinkedIn Profiler**' will give me good platform visibility.

When you are happy you have found some good keywords for you and your business, add them to your profile in the following areas:
a.   Headline
b.   About
c.   Experience

Potential Keyword List

Use this space to brainstorm some potential keywords and note the resu
This will help you to decide on which 2 or 3 to use.

....

....

....

....

....

....

....

....

....

....

....

....

....

....

CONNECTIONS

ow to make and handle connection requests is a vital part of LinkedIn. In y opinion, requests should always be personalised rather than sent without y context.

hen you send a connection request, LinkedIn prompts you to add a note d that is what you should do. It is important to let the person know why u would like to connect and/or how you met them. The only good reason t to personalise a request in my opinion, is when you are meeting people a live event where connecting is simply part of the networking process.

you are using the LinkedIn app, you might not see the prompt message to rsonalise a request initially. It is there, you just need to click on 'more' on e person's profile you are wanting to connect with, and you will then see e 'personalise request' option.

hen I receive a connection request that has a personalised note, I will read and often, this is enough for me to accept the connection. Sometimes ough, these messages can be a bit generic. If the message is generic, I will ok at the person's profile before deciding whether to accept.

I receive a request with no message, again, I will look at the person's ofile. If that person is of interest, I will then message them back asking y they would like to connect with me. Unfortunately, 90% of the time I t no reply, so I end up deleting the request.

me users will accept all requests as a way of growing their numbers, wever I see the LinkedIn platform as an engagement piece, so take a fferent approach as outlined above.

ice I accept a request, I will then message my new connection and ask w I can help. I may also add that if they are looking to sell to me, I will mediately delete them.

s possible to update your settings so that only you can see your connections. iis is to help prevent other users spamming your list of connections which s happened to me in the past.

Ultimately, how you manage and send connection requests is entirely up to you, but I find that using some discretion and professional courtesy tends to lead to more positive and beneficial long-term connections.

What are the different types of Connections?

- **1st Line Connections**: these are the people you are already connected to.
- **2nd Line Connections**: these are your connections, connections.
- **3rd Line Connections**: these are one step further away.

The free version of LinkedIn obviously has its limitations, one of which that you are unable to use InMails – the feature which allows you to send messages to people who are 3rd line connections.

Upgrading to the Premium version will unlock this function but I personally believe there is a flaw in this system. If a person does not know you, when they receive a message from you out of the blue it could be argued this is similar to a 'cold call'. Often this results in lack of acknowledgement or deletion of your request. When I send InMail messages to 3rd line connections with whom I have no previous history, I always get less than 10% engagement.

There is though, an easier way to access these 3rd line connections and this is by joining a group to which your target person belongs. You can then start a conversation within the group so that the person gets used to seeing your name. After that you can ask them if they'd like to connect. I have rarely been turned down with this approach and have a 90+% success rate.

YOUR PROFILE - Part A
Section 1

YOUR BANNER

is a well-researched fact that most people have a visual preference when it mes to absorbing information. A picture paints a thousand words as they y, so it's no surprise that a great banner can have a huge impact on those ewing your profile. A banner must therefore do its job effectively - but here is the banner and what is its job?

he banner is the large, horizontal space at the top of your profile page hich sits just behind your headshot. By clicking the pencil in the top right rner, you can edit this banner and upload an image.

he banner's main job is to let the viewer know they have landed on the rrect page. It should tell them what you do, thereby confirming they are the right track.

you are a photographer, for example, it is very tempting to have a beautiful ndscape photo for your banner image, but does it tell the viewer that you e a photographer?

milarly, if you are a speaker, you might use a shot of yourself speaking at event but, unless you add words to the banner, it can be unclear what you ecialise in and are able to speak about.

e know from research (**https://muckrack.com/blog/2020/07/14/how-clining-attention-spans-impact-your-social-media**) that viewers only end between 5 and 7 seconds on your profile before deciding. They will ther continue their search elsewhere or, if they like what they see, they will g deeper. We want everyone who lands on our profiles to dig deeper.

 Remember, all the 'good stuff' is hidden until the user clicks 'see more' on the third line of your **About** section so, if your banner doesn't do its job, they may never click on that 'see more' link and you will have lost a potential client.

I have seen some very clever banners that have engaged me, but only because I already knew the person. If I hadn't known them then I would undoubtedly have left the profile after my 5 to 7 seconds, because I would have been unclear as to what they do.

LinkedIn users are busy people and don't have the time to spend guessing what it is that you do.

How then, can you achieve an attention-grabbing banner that does its job?

Well, there are a few ways and what's more, you can sometimes keep that 'clever' banner.

1. You can add words to your banner. In the example of the photographer I would suggest adding the word '**Photographer**' (or appropriate variation) in a prominent place. If that photographer has a niche (e.g. branding photography) then they could use those niche words too. Not only will the viewer then see the stunning landscape (which is an example of the photographer's work), they will understand immediately what the person on whose page they have landed, does.

   Adding text to banners is simple to do and there is free software readily available which will help with this. I personally use a software called Canva (**www.canva.com**) which has a free version with a default template already loaded for LinkedIn banners. This is incredibly beneficial because you know that when you've finished designing your banner and are adding it to your LinkedIn profile, it will be the correct size.

2. Choose an image that doesn't need words. Again, going back to the photographer, they could use an image containing a camera body and lens, for example. The viewer would instantly know they have arrived at the page of a photographer, though it would not confirm any particular skills or niche. These specifics could be added as text in the same way we've mentioned above.

3. Make sure your banner is optimised for mobile viewing. The reason being that when LinkedIn is viewed on a smartphone via the LinkedIn app, your headshot takes up substantially more space than on the desktop version. Less of your banner is therefore visible.

We know that pre-Covid, 65% of people used the LinkedIn mobile app, (for this and many other useful stats look here **https://www.omnicoreagency.com/linkedin-statistics**) which is a huge percentage of people you can't afford to be invisible to.

On desktop view, your headshot takes up roughly half the height of your banner but in mobile, this increases to three quarters of its height. When designing your banner, therefore, it is best to avoid putting anything vital around the left-hand area of your banner because it will simply get lost.

My advice is to upload your banner, view it on mobile, and then make any changes as needed.

Examples of 'good' and 'bad' banners

ake a moment to review the banners of some of your connections and note here what, in your opinion, makes these good or bad.

....

....

....

....

....

....

....

Banner Ideas

Use this space to jot down any ideas you have for your banner. Includ
thoughts on images, style, layout and text. This helps to make the desi
process more straightforward when you come to fleshing it out.

....

....

....

....

....

....

....

....

....

....

....

....

....

....

....

Section 2

YOUR HEADSHOT

Your headshot is another visual element and is of key importance. Adding a headshot seems simple enough but is an area that users frequently overlook, especially when it comes to choosing the right shot.

LinkedIn is a professional business platform, so you should use a professional-looking headshot. There are plenty of photographers who can do this for you, and I would always recommend using one. Whilst cameras in smartphones are constantly improving, it is difficult to replicate the lighting and equipment a professional photographer would use.

A headshot is exactly what the name suggests and comprises a close-up image of your head and shoulders, ideally against a plain background with a smile facing into the page. Photographers will do these separately or as part of a branding shoot and once you have one, I would suggest using it on all your online profiles. The reason for this is that your headshot forms part of your branding, and branding and its consistency, are vital to your business.

Though it may seem costly to use a professional photographer, the investment is well worth it. We know that these headshots gain 14 times more engagement than a "casual shot" (see previous stats link) so it is key when it comes to attracting new clients. If you want people to spend money with you then look professional, and smile!

There is a school of thought which suggests certain industries do not benefit from a professional headshot. In the creative world, for example, I know many who feel it is more important for their personality to be on show, rather than a 'stuffy' posed shot. Ultimately it is your choice and is personal preference.

Whilst the figures show that a professional shot increases your engagement, that doesn't mean you need to wear a suit and tie. If you are looking smart and portraying a professional image, your headshot can work just as effectively.

The most important thing to consider is how your photo represents you. It must show the real you, not you from ten years ago, so that when you're meeting prospective clients in the flesh, they immediately know who you are. This is vital to your professional credibility.

If your headshot is out of date, change it. You don't want people doubting you from the off.

To edit your headshot:

1. Click on 'me' to the right of the top toolbar and select 'view profile'.
2. From your profile page, click on your image in the circle at the top left. This will open another window.
3. In the bottom right of this window there is an edit button with a pencil above it.
4. Click this and upload your new photo which you can then crop to fit the space.

Section 3

YOUR HEADLINE

When originally released by the HR world, Linked In was little more than an online CV and remained that way for years. Therefore, all the platform required was your job title. Now that is no longer the case and in fact, it is no longer about you as we discussed earlier on. It is all about your audience.

Your headline (the paragraph that sits beneath your name which is visible to viewers when you comment or interact with other posts), is used to hook your potential clients. The best strategy to create a 'winning' headline is to ask a question that gets a 'yes' from your target audience.

For example, as LinkedIn is my specialism, I would use a headline like:

"Looking for a LinkedIn specialist to help you with your profile and turn it into a lead generator? As a LinkedIn profiler I can assist!"

The question is one I want a 'yes' from and, as the potential client will have found me from a search or recommendation, a 'no' to this question wouldn't make any sense. I would presume they have looked me up for this very purpose.

With a 'yes', it is affirmation that they are looking for someone who can help them. A 'yes' also has a psychological effect. If someone says 'yes' they are generally in a positive mood and thus more likely to continue saying yes.

If someone answers 'no' to this question, I can be certain there would be no benefit from connecting - although for 20% of my clients, leads are not what they are after. What they are looking for is a new job or to get their profile up to date so that they can build relationships and increase their credibility.

So, the question affirms that potential clients are in the right place and are more likely to engage with your offer of help.

The headline currently comprises 220 characters which gives you plenty of room to ask that question, tell them you are the answer by putting credibility and outcomes statement in, and put in a call to action such as 'book a call now.'

As a tip, I change mine regularly to challenge the algorithm and keep fresh.

Potential Headlines

Use this space to brainstorm a few headlines you could use. Keep a note of any effect on your statistics so that you can narrow down what is working and what is not.

....

....

....

....

....

....

....

....

....

....

Section 4

YOUR ABOUT SECTION

<u>The first 3 lines</u>

ng with your banner, headshot, and headline, the first three lines of your
out section will be visible to the viewer, and the same premise applies.
 must write your About section content for your potential client, not for
rself.

ve a friendly bet with people that in these 3 lines they will have used 'I,
or me'. In fact, it is often in the first sentence if not the first word!

ne has the word '**you**' regularly in those 3 lines because I want them to be
aged and click on '**...show more**'.

en we only have a limited time to engage the viewer (5-7 seconds), these
s need to affirm you are the person they are looking for or that you
oly what they need. It should also demonstrate that you are interested in
n and not just the sale.

ou have been successful with your banner, headshot, headline and the
 3 lines of your About section, then there is no reason for a potential
nt not to click on '**...see more**'.

 worth remembering though, that with millions of people using the
kedIn platform, you are unlikely to be the only search result they return.
 therefore crucial to make sure that these top 4 sections are the best you
 make them.

 that the viewer has clicked on the '**...see more**' button, it will open up
 About section which then flows into the rest of your profile. It's time
hine!

 a note of caution: subtlety is key. Content that is too 'salesy' tends to put
ntial new clients off.

Just using your job title is not advisable in the opening of this section, you can include and expand on it.

Here, for example, is a great way to start your About section:

"**Would you like your LinkedIn profile to generate more leads? As th** **LinkedIn profiler with 15 years' experience, I can show you how you c** **spend less time but get better results on LinkedIn.**"

First 3-line ideas

Use this space to think of a few ways to tell your viewers what you d without focusing on yourself. Remember, it's about them.

....

....

....

....

....

....

....

....

....

....

....

YOUR PROFILE - Part B
Main Profile Elements

YOUR ABOUT SECTION

aving attracted the viewer with a great top section, now you can demonstrate at you are indeed the right person for your potential customer. The body your About section is the perfect place to start.

this area you have a maximum of 2,600 characters to showcase your skills cluding the first three lines) which means that from line four onwards, u can really add value to your offering.

this section include relevant achievements, current responsibilities and y numerical results that demonstrate your capability. Figures are great to e in this section as we know that people are drawn to proven results.

ake sure though, that it all relates to your current offering and not a past le. This is a very easy mistake to make, especially when you haven't used nkedIn for a while, but if you don't keep this up to date, it will be obvious your viewer and likely to have a negative impact.

so, the layout is crucial. If it is just line after line of text, then it will t people off. My suggestion is to ensure that there is white space and, if evant, have some bullet points to emphasise certain parts. You can also e sub-headings.

vo ideas that I use and teach are:

Add some social proof and
A call to action

ese are now explained in more detail.

Social Proof

Reviews and recommendations from previous clients are great examples social proof. Try to include a testimonial from a respected source. Someo saying that you do a great job will elevate the whole section. You can also u industry certifications. Again, this shows that you are dedicated and capab all of which will help with potential new clients.

Call to Action

A call to action is when you make it easy for your viewer to take the ne step. On websites these are typically buttons such as 'Contact Us' or 'Mo Information', but these are not available on LinkedIn. What you can though, is make sure you are offering easy ways for viewers to reach out you and encourage new visitors to do so.

An example would be:

'Contact me now for a free consultation' - followed by your email address

It is also okay to make this stand out by putting it in capitals.

I would not use a link to your website or put your phone number in this 'C to Action' as these are less likely to get engagement. People are comfortab using email so give them the easy option.

Use the next couple of pages to make some notes and jot down ideas f your About section. Remember to include the all important Social Pro and Calls to Action.

Content Ideas for my About section
(Including Social Proof and Calls to Action)

TONY K SILVER

TOP TIP !

FEATURED SECTION

w I come to a top tip!

ı can add more to your About section by using the Featured option
luding:

Posts

Articles

Links

Media

:his section (which you can access from the '**Add Section**' button at the
of your profile) you can upload different things such as say a PDF of top
, interesting facts, or a link to a webpage. You can also add videos, pin
ortant posts, and highlight your latest article.

the Featured section is part of the engine and algorithm, sending
vers away from your Profile to other websites is safe because they will
ɔmatically be returned.

en you upload a video, LinkedIn will ask where on your desktop the
ɔ is stored. This is because LinkedIn does not like YouTube and prefers
not to send people there. The best way around this is to save a copy of
r videos to your desktop or in the cloud. That way you won't be sending
r new LinkedIn viewers to You Tube - which keeps the algorithm happy!

ɔuld advise that the first two or three items you add here are directly
vant to you and your business because most people will only look at
e couple of items and not scroll further.

I therefore recommend the first three items in your Featured section be:

- Your latest article
- A 30-45 second video introduction
- A link to your website

There are two advantages to making sure you utilise this section. First gives the viewer more items to immerse themselves in, but more importan LinkedIn will index you for doing this and the more indexing points y get, the more chance you have of being found in searches.

Featured Section ideas

Use this space to consider how you can best use your Featured section

....

....

....

....

....

....

....

....

....

....

Main Profile Elements

YOUR ACTIVITY

This forms part of your main Profile page and in addition, utilised correctly, you will gain more indexing points, thus increasing the likelihood of appearing in searches.

The 'Your Activity' section contains two types of activity: **Posts** and **Articles**. These are both indexed by LinkedIn and are a great way to show you are an expert in your field by sharing brilliant content.

Comments you make on other users' posts will also feature here so it can help demonstrate your commitment to working with others and on the LinkedIn platform itself.

Further, you can add images and video as well as downloadable documents to a post which gives the viewer more content.

Not only that but it's another opportunity for LinkedIn to index you, so I would always recommend making sure you are active both on your own profile as well as those of fellow users.

ARTICLES

Articles are effectively LinkedIn's Blog and as such you can repurpose a blog into an article.

My suggestion is that you create your Blog/Article in a Word document, put in a folder on your desktop and then add the images. From this folder you upload it to your website and about a week later, cut and paste it into LinkedIn's Articles template. Make sure you change at least one image and some words though, otherwise LinkedIn won't index you as highly.

A quick note on images – make sure that you are using images from either your own collection or ones for which you own the copyright.

You can access a huge number of royalty-free images from sites such **Pixabay** (www.pixabay.com) and **Unsplash** (www.unsplash.com).

Or if you use Google, ensure the Creative Commons Licenses is checked. This can be found in '**Tools**', under '**Usage Rights**'.

Before using any images though, make sure you have read all the applicable copyright licenses, especially if you are adding images to products that you sell. **If you're unsure, don't use the image.**

The format I use for an article is as follows:

- I write between 600 - 800 words.
- I add in a few images to break up the text and make it more visually appealing.
- I include an eye-catching image at the top.
- And I aim for an engaging headline. "**My Latest Article**" is not going to get you many readers.
- I always put a '**call to action**' at the end. It's so important to let people know what you would like them to do next or you could have just wasted an opportunity.
- Sometimes I add video which can be a good idea but be careful not to upset the flow for the reader.

You can find the '**Article**' option at the top of your Home page.

I would recommend adding one article per month.

POSTS

These are smaller than articles and I aim to do 2 or 3 a week. They come in two guises - long and short form - with short form being the most popular.

As of July 2021, the number of characters available increased from 1,300 to 3,000 and with the average word being 4.8 letters long, that is a maximum of around 625 words.

With **long form** it's always good to let people know at the beginning how long your post will take to read, so if they don't have time, they can save it. As a rule of thumb, I use a reading speed of 225 words per minute, so a 625-word long form post would take just under 3 minutes to read.

Short form posts need to be at least 3 lines long and should be engaging. You can ask a question or start a discussion to help you get some interaction. The template is straightforward to use so a short form post shouldn't take too long to compose.

I believe that people are visually orientated. Viewers will almost always spot a good strong image, so I usually make sure to add one to my posts. (See comments on images in previous and following section).

Alongside your activity, it is essential to interact with other posts and articles as they come through your feed. These you can choose to **Like**, **Comment** (at least 4 words, but 13 is the sweet spot) or **Share** and it is good to do this at least once a day. LinkedIn sees it as activity, which helps you.

A note of caution on using the **Share** function though:

As of February 2021, LinkedIn sees 'sharing' as duplicate content and therefore reduces its reach. A way around this is to get the original author involved in your sharing and that does the trick.

IMAGES

As mentioned above, viewers tend react to a strong image, so I use the same sites as previously referenced to add one to my posts. Often, I will use editing software to add words to these images so that they deliver their message in an even more powerful way.

Canva (www.canva.com) is great for this.

DOCUMENTS

Also to be found at the top of your Home page is the document sharing. You will see it in the Post template after the image and video icons. Here you can upload documents you would like to share. The viewer can then download them as a pdf directly, so it's a great place to give more value.

VIDEO

Video on LinkedIn is very powerful and can increase your reach...but it can also be less effective if you make it too long.

From my experience something in the 30 seconds to 1 minute area are about right. In fact, you will see your reach reduced once the video goes over 2 minutes.

Also, make sure you add subtitles. This is because by default, videos on LinkedIn are set to play on mute. It's very straightforward to add subtitles to your video. I use **www.getsubly.com** which I find easy to use and the results are pretty accurate.

If you're using videos, make sure that you have them stored on your desktop or in the cloud. As previously mentioned, LinkedIn does not like external links, especially those leading to YouTube. I find the best solution is to record them in Zoom which automatically stores them in my 'documents' in a folder named Zoom.

REACH

This is very important. The '**reach**' your post/article/video achieves will determine the number of people who get to see them.

Reach can be affected by various things in both a positive and negative way. These factors do change over time when LinkedIn update their algorithm but the following activities are good indicators of each:

As of July 2021:

Positive Indicators	Negative Indicators
Video 20 - 40%	External links
Documents 40 - 60%	Sharing
Images 10 - 20%	Polls

Activity Ideas

e this area to make some notes about what kind of activity you plan to
. It is also useful to note the impact of each of your actions so that you
can see what is working.

....

....

....

....

....

....

....

....

....

....

....

....

....

....

Activity Impact

....

....

....

....

....

....

....

....

....

....

....

....

....

....

....

....

Main Profile Elements

YOUR EXPERIENCE

his is a section that many see as a leftover from the days when your profile
. LinkedIn was just an online CV, however it is still very relevant today. It
another area where you can promote yourself which adds to your overall
esence and indexing on LinkedIn.

usually suggest adding 3-4 lines of text here outlining your achievements,
sponsibilities, and relevant figures (if you have them). How you made or
ved the company money, for example, is an excellent way to demonstrate
ur skills.

this section you can also add media by way of links and uploads in the
ne way as you can within your Featured section. In fact, you can use the
ne ones again.

r your previous roles it's not as important to provide a lot of detail, unless
ese are pertinent to your current offering.

EDUCATION

e Education section is not considered to be useful for majority of LinkedIn
ers. As something that formed a large part of the platform when it was
nply an online CV, I find that unless you are a young person looking for
rk, the benefits to completing this section are limited.

a side note though, you can search for users via their educational
ablishments which could be a good way to connect with those you were
university with, for example.

LICENSES AND CERTIFICATION

is has now become its own section, and many may have missed it, but if
u are in a role that dictates a need to pass examinations and/or apply for
enses to carry out your job legally, then adding these is a must.

The Licenses and Certification section can be found in the drop-down men under your headline at the top of your profile. If you select 'Add Sectio you will find the Licenses and Certification option. It has a straightforwa template, but you do need some exact details to complete it fully.

If I was looking to engage a professional who required a particul qualification, I would expect to see that noted on their profile. If they d not have this showing, I would be less likely to engage with them.

SKILLS AND ENDORSEMENTS

This section appeared when Microsoft took ownership of LinkedIn in 201 In my opinion, it doesn't really work.

Why?

Endorsing someone is so easy. It's just a click of a button - you don't ev have to know them – which, in my opinion renders the endorsement usele

When you land on a person's profile, LinkedIn will randomly throw up a b containing 4 skills that the person you have searched for has and will a you what their top skill is. You can click any of these skills, even if you a unknown to the person on whose profile you've landed.

In addition, LinkedIn allows you to add up to 50 skills and many people d (Including me at one stage!)

I have since learned that this section is a weak part of the LinkedIn platfo and now use the following strategy:

- I have only 10-12 core skills available that apply to my current compa Therefore, if people are given the choice and want to endorse me, th it will be for a key skill.
- I have also found that adding your keywords as a new skill helps yo results in the LinkedIn search.

Your profile page will only show 3 of these skills, defaulted by the high number of endorsements. You might not want these to be the 3 skills sho however, so there is an option to edit the default order.

List of key skills that need to be in this section

Make a note of the 10-12 key skills you would like to focus on. Choose those which are most relevant to your current career.

....

....

....

....

....

....

....

....

....

....

....

....

....

....

....

....

RECOMMENDATIONS

This is one of the most important parts of your profile.

It is where you add value to yourself and your offering, with social proof.

You can either ask someone to write a recommendation for you or one of your connections can volunteer. It's worth noting though, **recommendations** can only be done by **1st line connections**.

The process is easy. You fill in a simple template which is then sent to the person as a notification. In this template you will tell the person what you would like their recommendation to be for, which is important because it will ensure the recommendation is relevant. One of your connections can also offer a recommendation without being asked, simply by visiting your profile page and clicking '**Recommend**' in the '**More**' section. There will be the same template for them to complete.

It is generally recognised that we all have a fear of rejection (particularly us British), so asking someone to write a testimonial can feel uncomfortable. The LinkedIn process though, doesn't allow for rejection which is great news.

If someone doesn't want to write you a recommendation, then they simply don't return the form (although usually this happens because people forget). And, if you don't like the recommendation when it is returned, you can choose not to add it to your profile or ask them if they could amend it. This means that you have complete control over who gives you a recommendation and, to a certain extent, what it says.

I always recommend asking for four times the number of recommendations you need. This is because only two recommendations are visible on your profile without clicking '**see more**' and it is preferable for these two to be current (i.e., from the month you are in or the preceding month).

At present I am asking for 8 recommendations to receive the magic 2 and it's worth bearing in mind that once your review numbers get into double figures, you will be elevated above most other users.

research shows that the average number of reviews per profile is 5 and the
age age of a review is 2-3 years old! Therefore, if you have 10+ reviews
2 current ones, you are likely to win the battle in a search comparison.

t is social proof, you need to constantly ask for recommendations so that
 remain up to date. Other users will judge you based on the number you
 as well as when they were given.

't forget though that you don't need to post all of those you receive. If
want to you can ask the author to make an amendment or you can toggle
'show' button which will hide the recommendation from your profile.

 thing to be watchful of is doing recommendations in return for those
n. These will show up on both yours and your fellow user's feed and will
 contrived.

nd to recommend people whom I have paid for a service they have
vered, or people where I have witnessed their work. I don't often get
d to do a recommendation for others but will happily do so if I think
appropriate. If I have only just met them though, then I don't consider I
w enough about them to make a judgement and will not usually offer a
mmendation.

tio of 60/40 (received/given) is considered optimal, and I think that's
it right. I would also suggest aiming to add 2 recommendations to your
ile a month, although that does depend on your work and your clients.

ommendations don't just have to be given because of work, however.
u have provided value to someone in a 1:1 for example, it is perfectly
ptable to ask them to give you a recommendation.

ommendations are one of LinkedIn's badges of honour. Over 100
mmendations is the target. If you are actively adding to yours, then this
hievable. Having looked at over 10,000 profiles, I'm finding the average
ber of reviews to be between 3 and 5. So, even getting 10 reviews will
nitely set you apart.

The most important benefit of recommendations is as social proof. People buy based on reviews – I know I do on Amazon regularly – and if there lots of good reviews, I am comforted that my choice is sound, and I invariably make the purchase.

Social proof is everywhere, and we are continually engaged with it. If friend tells you that the latest film/book/game is great it will influence your buying decision in a positive way whereas one bad review, will put you off.

This is where the recommendation system on LinkedIn is so great because you have complete control over which recommendations your potential clients can see.

If you have delivered a good service, it is natural for people to respond your recommendation request in a positive way. This will make the viewer of your profile more likely to engage because they feel reassured you will do a good job.

People I could ask

Make a note of some people you could approach on LinkedIn who would be able to provide you with a recommendation.

....

....

....

....

....

....

....

ACCOMPLISHMENTS

his is not a standard section, but I feel it is one that you should add to your ofile as it provides another opportunity to showcase your skills.

hen you click **'Add Section'** from the top of your profile you will find ccomplishments' in the drop-down box. From there you will see a list of 8 bsections to choose from and I would suggest that you add 2 or 3 of these d populate.

;ain, this helps the viewer to confirm in their mind that they are looking the profile of someone who can help them.

doesn't take too long to add and populate these fields and, as it is a positive dition to your profile, I would suggest you include this section. Then you 1 add to it when you have another accomplishment under your wings. It free text so you can add in your own words here which is really beneficial.

a starting point I would recommend adding organisations you have •rked with, courses you have taken and projects you have worked on. All these will improve your credibility for the viewer and underline how you 1 help and support potential new clients.

<u>Content I could add into this section</u>

Use this area to brainstorm some accomplishments you could add.

....

....

....

....

....

....

GROUPS

This is one of the sections that got a little lost during the Microsoft takeov[er]. Up until 2016 it was one of the most useful sections on LinkedIn, but i[ts] effectiveness was diluted during and after the change of ownership.

Now though, Groups are starting to regain traction and are providi[ng] benefits to users (engagement, reach etc…) which means there are ma[ny] good reasons to join a group or run your own. This in itself can really he[lp] raise your profile.

There are thousands of groups you can join on LinkedIn and my suggesti[on] is to keep it to around a dozen so you can be active in 3 or 4 regular[ly]. Remember to check that the groups you choose to join are still acti[ve]. Many of them ceased to be used after 2016 but still show good numbers [of] members.

Being part of and active in a group is something you need to be doing to g[et] LinkedIn's attention (those good old algorithms) as well as the attention [of] other platform users. Groups are a great place to show your expertise so w[ith] that in mind, choose your groups well.

My suggestion is to join groups which are going to help elevate your stat[us] so you could consider ones that are geographically relevant to your offeri[ng]. Also, find those that are allied to your area of expertise as well as ones wh[ere] your ideal customers are likely to be.

Once you've chosen your groups, start to add to discussions and genera[lly] get involved. Groups provide a great opportunity to meet and connect w[ith] 3rd Line connections (see **Connection Request** section for details of wh[at] these and other connections are) and get them on board.

If you add to a discussion started by a 3rd line connection and mention th[eir] name by tagging them, they will become aware of you. You can also ask the[m] a direct question.

When you subsequently ask them to connect, your chances of acceptance a[re] then greatly increased.

is also a good idea to create your own group to which you can invite ~~ients and associates. This provides them with additional value, which will ~~rich your relationship with them.

~~lways make sure you advise clients, associates and potential clients to turn ~~e notification settings in Groups to 'see all posts' or they may miss some ~~ your valuable information and content.

Group Ideas

~~se this area to note down the types of Groups it would be beneficial for you to join along with some ideas around creating your own Group.

....

....

....

....

....

....

....

....

....

....

....

SEARCHES

LinkedIn is a very large database. At the time of writing (Q2 2021), the
were some 774 million registered user accounts. Of these, around 32 millic
are based in the UK.

LinkedIn claims to be present in 200 countries (which is phenomen
considering there only 197 countries in the world recognised by the Unit
Nations), but it does illustrate the point that LinkedIn has a very wide reac

There are 2 parts to the search element of LinkedIn: to search for peop
and to be found yourself.

Let's take searching for others first and see how to do it effectively in tl
free version of the platform. You will soon discover that there are some goc
filters available to assist you here without the need to upgrade to a pa
version.

When searching, most people start with a generic search term and are p
off when it returns a large (6 or 7 figure) number of results. A far mo
effective way of searching in the standard platform is:

- Firstly, be more targeted by using a **'Boolean'** search. This means usi
  '+' or '-' and other symbols in the search box along with the keywor
  to narrow down your results.

  For example: **Accountant + Partner** targets much more effectively.

  You can also put a search request between speech marks. This mea
  it will only pick out an answer with those exact words which aga
  produces a much more targeted result.

- Next there are the filters. These appear across the top of your Sear
  results. My suggestion is to click **'all filters'** which gives you 10 filte
  that you can apply:

  * Connections Level
  * Connections of Locations
  * Current Companies

* Past Companies
* Industry
* Profile
* Language
* Schools
* Contact Interests
* Name and Job Title

A normal search I use is:

Connection level = 2, Location = local area, Industry = (what I am searching for) and Job Title

Playing with the filters will drastically reduce the number of search results you receive and using the method above, generally returns a list of below 100 matches. I then look at each individual result and contact those that interest me. If they have added their phone number, I will call them, otherwise, I send a message.

You can see, you can get good results just by tweaking your Search criteria using the filters without investing in the upgraded version of LinkedIn.

Search Terms

this space to jot down a few search terms and keywords you could use to gain the most benefit.

....

....

....

....

....

Other LinkedIn Platform Highlights

(all accessed from the left side panel on your home page)

WHO HAS VIEWED MY PROFILE?

Contrary to popular belief, you do not need to buy LinkedIn Premium make valuable use of this feature. All you need is a bit of discipline and make sure you look at '**who has viewed your profile**', twice a day.

In the standard free version of LinkedIn, you will see the last 5 viewers chronological order so if you check this area in the morning and again in afternoon you will see those most recent views. In my opinion, any pro view over 36 hours old, is probably a bit cold.

Some of your viewers will be 1st line connections, and some will be line. Ignore these two for now and click on any 2nd line connections. If person is of interest, then contact them either by phone or message.

NOTE: This is not considered to be cold calling because the viewer shown an interest in you by looking at your profile. When I reach ou often ask what it was that drew them to my profile and if there's anyth I can do to help. I will also suggest a 1:1 meeting and often, as they are ones who looked me up, they agree to have a chat.

SAVED ITEMS

There is a Saved Items section (currently being upgraded to My Ite where all the saved posts, articles etc… from your feed are kept. You will this in your dashboard on your profile home page.

If you're not sure how to save things, it's a simple process:

- All the items in your feed have 3 dots in the top right corner. W you click on these dots the first option you have is to 'save' that ite saving items has 2 uses:

You can save items to look at later.

Your viewers can save items if they don't have time to read your content initially. For this reason, I would always recommend putting a 'guide' reading time on longer posts. I usually use a figure based on 225 words per minute as a rough rule of thumb to calculate the reading time.

EVENTS

The Events section is in the left-hand menu on your LinkedIn home page. If you click the '+' button to open the template, you can create a new event and see those you've already created.

The template asks you to import some images, add text and make choices such as is the event public or private. It will then allow you to add your event link to Eventbrite or the hosting URL.

Once created you can share the event from within the actual event via a LinkedIn post or share it to other social media such as Twitter.

THE TABS

It is worth getting to know all the tabs, not just the ones that you use.

The Tabs can be found at the very top of your Home screen and are, from left to right:

Home – this accesses your main feed and is where you can create posts and articles.

My Network- here you can access your connections, see those who have sent you requests along with requests you have sent yourself. You can also manage your connections from here.

If the number of people in your sent list grows too big or gets too old, LinkedIn may suspect you of spamming people. If you have more than 20 unanswered connection requests therefore, and particularly if some are over one month old, withdraw them. If you wish to try again, you can resend the request in 3 weeks' time.

- **Jobs** – this is a section for jobseekers and will provide a list of availab. jobs.

- **Messages** – this is a list of messages sent and received and is distribute in chronological order.

- **Notifications**- lists all your notifications. You should look at the regularly because there are often actions to be taken.

- **Me** – this is where you can access your profile, settings, company pa and other items.

- **Work** – this option opens a sub-menu which contains mostly HR too but it is also where the **Groups** icon sits. In my opinion, accessing t **Groups** section from here provides it in a more useful layout.

- **Advertise** – this is where you can access the LinkedIn advertisi options.

SETTINGS AND PRIVACY

The Settings and Privacy options are accessible from the "**Me**" tab, and und this you will find multiple headings. My advice is to have a look around a check the settings on the parts of the platform that you use.

Changing your Settings is clear from the layout, and the options that a available for each setting are given.

I would recommend having a look at '**Visibility**' and the sub sections 'E Your Public Profile'. If you click on this, it will show your profile as appears to the public (new viewers). I would always suggest removing t numbers from '**Edit Your Custom URL**' at the top right of this section make your profile link more professional and easier for new connections remember.

The next sub-heading I would suggest you look at is '**Profile Viewi Options**'. This is where you can change how others see you when you on the platform and can be especially useful when looking at other profi will automatically show the default setting, and it is best to leave it on here, but if you want to do some market research (on other users for example), you can go into Anonymous mode (option 3).

This will mean you are identified as a 'LinkedIn member' (rather than your name), but be aware that when you use this mode you cannot see who has viewed your profile, so ensure you turn it off when you have finished.

I always tell my clients to spend a good 30 minutes looking at all the Setting and Privacy options, especially the ones below:

Your email address - can you still access all the listed ones and if not, delete those that are no longer relevant.

Who can see your connections? Do you want all your connections having access?

People also viewed - do you want others/new clients to see this list of who could be competitors?

MORE

This appears on your First Line connections profile as a dropdown menu and is well worth having a look at.

The options are.

Share profile in a message - **Share xxxxx profile via message.**

Save to PDF - **Save xxxxx profile to PDF.**

Give **Kudos.**

Request a recommendation - **Request xxxxx recommendation.**

Recommend - **Write a recommendation for xxxxx.**

Unfollow - **Unfollow xxxxxx.**

Remove Connection - **Remove your connection to xxxxx.**

Report / Block.

Most are self-explanatory but **Kudos** is something people do not notice, and I think is a nice addition.

KUDOS

This is a relatively new part of the platform and is a brilliant way to show appreciation to others. The only downside is there are currently no metric so you cannot see how many you have received and sent each month.

From the 'More' dropdown list click on 'Kudos' and you will be given choice of 10 cards with content such as "Thank You" and the person's nam

Clicking 'next' allows you to personalise the card and add any hashtag before you publish it. The person to whom you are giving kudos will receiv a notification and it will appear on their feed. It will also show in your fee so is a great addition to LinkedIn, it's just a shame there are no metrics.

Kudos Ideas

Make some notes of who you can give kudos to and why.

....

....

....

....

....

....

....

....

....

CREATOR MODE

s is a switchable mode that appears in your dashboard unannounced. It
1ore obvious on the App version, and it allows you to change the way
r profile looks. Using this mode is optional as it may not be for everyone.

: Creator Mode:

Allows you to add a 'Cover Story' (see App section that follows).

Allows you to highlight 5 areas by adding hashtags just under your
headline.

Show the number of followers you have – this is seen before your
number of connections, again under the headline.

Rearranges your profile section to put **Featured** and **Activity** at the top.
The Activity section is also slightly bigger here than the standard view.

Moves your dashboard to the top (remember only you can see this).

THE LINKEDIN APP

kedIn has an App and although it is a cut-down of the desktop version,
ill has several great functions. That being said, I personally believe that
editing is best done via the desktop version.

App has some extras though, and these are worth exploring as they can
eneficial.

ngs you can do on the App are:

Scanner

LinkedIn App has a scanner and QR code for people to scan. This is
e useful in smaller networking groups where you can 'scan' each other's
codes for speed.

QR code will take you directly to that person's profile where you can
ask to connect in the usual way. One additional benefit of using the QR
: and scanner is hygiene.

You can swap details with someone without touching their business c
which has become a valid concern during the recent pandemic.

The scanner can be found in the search window at the top of the scr
on the right-hand side (where there are box shapes). If you click here
scanner opens by default.

Alternatively, it can be found in the "**My Network**" tab at the bottom
the screen.

Messages

The App also allows you to send voice or video messages rather than
text, which can be useful. Sometimes it's easier to use voice, particular
you have a long message and similarly, sending a video message can o
be more powerful.

To access this feature, go to the person you want to message and p
the message button. You will see the usual box at the bottom inviting
to '**write a message**' but if you look to the right of this box, you will
a **microphone option**. Pressing and holding this enables you to recor
message, for which the recipient will receive an alert. The voice mess
also remains in your audit list with that person so you can access it as w

On the far left of the message box you will see a '+' symbol which, w
pressed, opens a sub menu and the video option is on the top line h
Selecting the video option opens the screen for you to record your mess

Make sure you reverse your camera so that it is pointing towards you
press '**record**'. Once you have finished your message, press '**record**' agai
end. When you've finished you will be shown the video which you can t
choose to send.

I personally find receiving a voice or video message preferable. It can rem
the lack of understanding or confusion that sometimes occurs in simple t
It can be a more efficient way to deliver your meaning and is worth try
out.

cent additions in the first half of 2021 include the option to record a 10 cond audio clip which is accessed by clicking the loudspeaker next to your me. This was originally added to help people with the pronunciation of ur name, but as it is 10 seconds long, it can be used as a second headline.

nother addition is the Creator Mode video recording which allows you to eate a 30 second video 'Cover Story'. This video is previewed when people d on your profile by the showing of a 3 second muted video where your adshot is. If the user then clicks your headshot, the video will open in full w. This video also plays audio so can be a great tool to give visitors to your ofile more information about yourself and your business.

VIDEO CALLING ON LINKEDIN

nkedIn is rolling out video calls via the message feature. If you look at any your **messages** you will see a **video icon** at the top right. If you then open s you will see two options:

Send instant meeting.
Schedule meeting for later.

u then have the option to use LinkedIn, Teams or Zoom.

hen you enter the meeting you will have to set up your camera and crophone permissions but other than that, it's done!

you want to check if a person you're wishing to meet is online, simply visit ir profile and if they have a small, solid green circle on their headshot, n you know they are online.

e addition of video calling/conferencing is a bold move by LinkedIn, but e that I think is going to be very exciting to watch.

REVIEWS ON YOUR SERVICES

Once you have included your **Services** from the **Add** section button, (have you not done it yet?), choose 10 of these Services. This will then enable you to ask for up to 20 reviews. Simply choose a **service** and ask (invite) connection if they will provide you with a review for this particular service.

As you start getting these reviews back you will build up an overall star rating, which is beneficial when it comes to promoting and marketing yourself and your business.

FINESSE YOUR FEED

A recent survey stated that we only spend around 25-30 seconds scanning down our feed which means we will only see 12-15 posts. If though you scroll down to the 25th through to the 30th posts in your feed, you will find connections you've not heard from in a while. Take a moment engage with these connections twice in the following 48 hours and they will automatically feature as part of the 10-15% of posts you regularly see.

Another way to 'finesse your feed' is to refresh the page. This gives you different set of posts to browse. Additionally, the posts displayed to you the LinkedIn mobile app are also different, effectively given you the chance to see three alternative streams in your feed.

Final summary

adly we have reached the end of our whistle stop tour of LinkedIn, which I ope has illustrated many of the benefits this platform can offer. In addition the tips I have shared, I'd like to think that hearing my story has also spired you to use LinkedIn more effectively and to implement some of ese strategies so that you too can achieve your goals.

inkedIn is a powerful Personal and Professional Business Tool and is mething I believe most businesspeople benefit from using. It does work st if kept up to date though, so if you are not able to do this, it can be a od option to close your profile so that potential clients are not seeing out date information.

r those of you who want to create some noise and generate leads, then plying what is contained in this book will help you to get closer to an fective profile that stands out from your competitors.

nce you've achieved an effective profile, qualified leads and increased sales ten follow.

wish you all the best of luck on your journey and would love to hear how u get on.

Tony K Silver

linkedin.com/in/tonyksilver
www.solidsilversolutions.com

WORKSHOP NOTES

WORKSHOP NOTES

WORKSHOP NOTES

WORKSHOP NOTES

WORKSHOP NOTES

WORKSHOP NOTES

Lightning Source UK Ltd.
Milton Keynes UK
UKHW011011261121
394640UK00011B/927